Easy Layer-Cake Quilts 2

MORE SIMPLE QUILTS FROM 10" SQUARES

Barbara Groves and Mary Jacobson
of Me and My Sister Designs

Martingale
Create with Confidence

Easy Layer-Cake Quilts 2:
More Simple Quilts from 10" Squares
© 2018 by Barbara Groves and Mary Jacobson

Martingale®
19021 120th Ave. NE, Ste. 102
Bothell, WA 98011-9511 USA
ShopMartingale.com

Printed in Hong Kong

23 22 21 20   8 7 6 5 4

Library of Congress Cataloging-in-Publication Data is available upon request.

ISBN: 978-1-60468-946-4

MISSION STATEMENT

We empower makers who use fabric and yarn to make life more enjoyable.

CREDITS

PUBLISHER AND
CHIEF VISIONARY OFFICER
Jennifer Erbe Keltner

CONTENT DIRECTOR
Karen Costello Soltys

MANAGING EDITOR
Tina Cook

ACQUISITIONS EDITOR
Karen M. Burns

TECHNICAL EDITOR
Ellen Pahl

COPY EDITOR
Durby Peterson

DESIGN MANAGER
Adrienne Smitke

PRODUCTION MANAGER
Regina Girard

COVER AND
INTERIOR DESIGNER
Kathy Kotomaimoce

PHOTOGRAPHER
Brent Kane

ILLUSTRATOR
Lisa Lauch

Contents

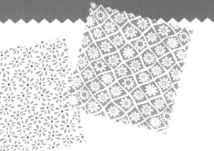
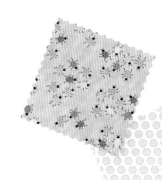

Introduction

Layer Cakes! Layer Cakes! For us there's no better name for a fabric precut. It's our favorite dessert in the form of fabric—and it doesn't get much better than that!

So, what is a Layer Cake? *Layer Cake* is a term trademarked by Moda Fabrics to describe a bundle of 42 precut fabric squares that measure 10" × 10". Each Layer Cake usually contains at least one square of each fabric from an entire collection.

This book is a follow-up to our previous book, *Easy Layer-Cake Quilts.* As in that book, there are 11 projects made specifically for using Layer Cake precuts. All of the quilts are designed for confident beginners and beyond. None are overly time intensive, and most can be completed in a few days. For best results, just be sure to read the "quilt recipes" carefully before cutting.

Now you can have even more Layer Cake fun. Let's get baking!

~Barb and Mary

Happy Dance

FINISHED QUILT: 78½" × 78½" • FINISHED BLOCK: 8" × 8"

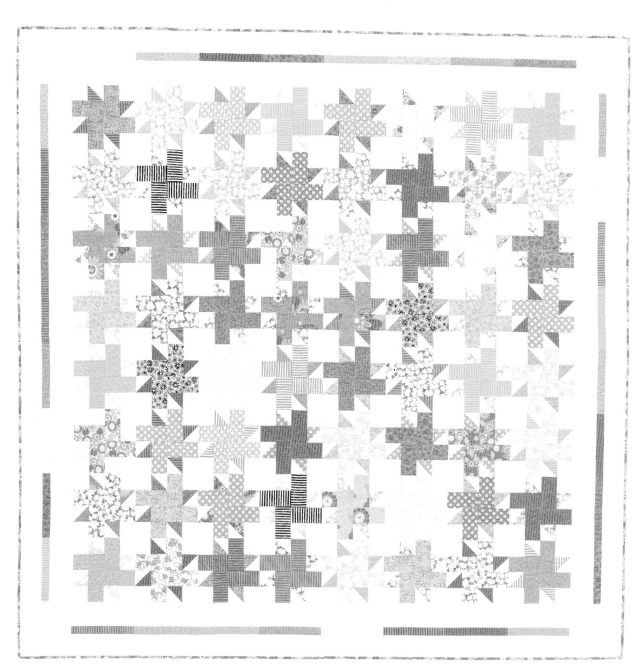

Made with the Happy fabric line by Me and My Sister Designs

You'll need two Layer Cakes, a solid fabric, and some binding to make this happy quilt recipe. It's the perfect size for a picnic in the park. Just add sunshine.

Materials

Yardage is based on 42"-wide fabric.

3¾ yards of white print for blocks and borders
64 squares, 10" × 10", of assorted prints for blocks and pieced border*
⅔ yard of multicolored print for binding
7⅛ yards of fabric for backing
85" × 85" square of batting

A Moda Layer Cake contains 42 squares, 10" × 10".

Cutting

All measurements include ¼" seam allowances. Refer to the cutting guide below when cutting the Layer Cake squares.

From the white print, cut:
1 strip, 7½" × 42"; crosscut into 4 squares, 7½" × 7½"
13 strips, 3½" × 42"
10 strips, 2⅞" × 42"; crosscut into 128 squares, 2⅞" × 2⅞"
16 strips, 2½" × 42"; crosscut into 256 squares, 2½" × 2½"

From *each* of the print 10" squares, cut:
4 rectangles, 2½" × 4½" (256 total)
2 squares, 2⅞" × 2⅞" (128 total)

From the *remainder of 32* print 10" squares, cut:
1 rectangle, 1½" × 8½" (32 total)

From the multicolored print, cut:
9 strips, 2¼" × 42"

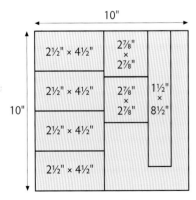

Cutting guide

Making the Blocks

Use a ¼"-wide seam allowance and a small stitch length throughout. Press all seam allowances open, unless otherwise noted.

1 For each block, choose the following:
- 2 white squares, 2⅞" × 2⅞"
- 2 matching print squares, 2⅞" × 2⅞"
- 4 matching print rectangles, 2½" × 4½"
- 4 white squares, 2½" × 2½"

2 Draw a diagonal line from corner to corner on the wrong side of the white 2⅞" squares. With right sides together, layer a marked 2⅞" square and a print 2⅞" square. Stitch ¼" from each side of the drawn line. Cut apart on the marked line and press to make a half-square-triangle unit. Make four units measuring 2½" square.

Make 4 units,
2½" × 2½".

3 Arrange and sew a half-square-triangle unit, a white 2½" square, and a print 2½" × 4½" rectangle together as shown to make a unit. Make four units measuring 4½" square.

Make 4 units,
4½" × 4½".

4 Join the four units into a block as shown. Make 64 blocks measuring 8½" square, including seam allowances.

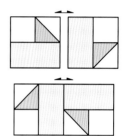 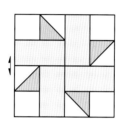

Make 64 blocks,
8½" × 8½".

Assembling the Quilt Top

1 Referring to the quilt assembly diagram on page 9, arrange the blocks into eight rows of eight blocks each. Sew the blocks into rows, and then sew the rows together. The quilt center should measure 64½" square, including seam allowances.

2 Join the 13 white 3½" × 42" strips together end to end. From this length, cut eight strips, 64½" long.

3 Piece eight print 1½" × 8½" rectangles together end to end to make a border strip. Make four border strips measuring 1½" × 64½".

Make 4 strips, 1½" × 64½".

4 Sew a pieced border strip between two white 3½" × 64½" strips as shown. Make four pieced borders measuring 7½" × 64½", including seam allowances.

Make 4 pieced borders, 7½" × 64½".

5 Sew a pieced border to the left and right sides of the quilt center.

6 Sew a white 7½" square to each end of the remaining two pieced borders. Join these borders to the top and bottom of the quilt. The completed quilt top should measure 78½" square.

Finishing

For more information on any of the finishing steps, go to ShopMartingale.com/HowtoQuilt for free downloadable instructions.

1 Layer the backing, batting, and quilt top; baste the layers together. Hand or machine quilt as desired. Our quilt is machine quilted with petal motifs in the white squares and leaf shapes in the prints and borders.

2 Trim and square up the quilt. Make the binding using the multicolored 2¼"-wide strips and attach it to the quilt.

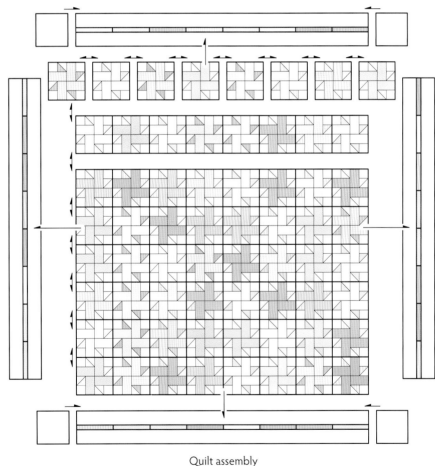

Quilt assembly

A Slice of Cake

FINISHED QUILT: 52" × 52" • FINISHED BLOCK: 8" × 8"

Made with the Blushing Peonies fabric line by Robin Pickens

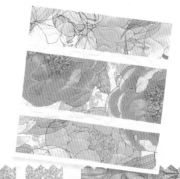

Cutting a Layer Cake into slices can be so much fun! Slice your favorite Layer Cake and add a solid color "frosting" between the layers. Just about any Layer Cake you love will work in this recipe.

Materials

Yardage is based on 42"-wide fabric.

25 squares, 10" × 10", of assorted prints for blocks*
1⅓ yards of white solid for blocks, sashing, and inner border
⅝ yard of green floral for outer border
½ yard of green print for binding
3¼ yards of fabric for backing
58" × 58" square of batting

A Moda Layer Cake contains 42 squares, 10" × 10".

Cutting

All measurements include ¼" seam allowances. Keep like prints together.

From *each* of the print 10" squares, cut:
2 rectangles, 2½" × 8½" (50 total)
1 rectangle, 3½" × 8½" (25 total)

From the white solid, cut:
3 strips, 8½" × 42"; crosscut into:
   50 rectangles, 1" × 8½"
   20 rectangles, 1½" × 8½"
10 strips, 1½" × 42"

From the green floral, cut:
5 strips, 3¼" × 42"

From the green print, cut:
6 strips, 2¼" × 42"

Making the Blocks

Use a ¼"-wide seam allowance and a small stitch length throughout. Press all seam allowances open, unless otherwise noted.

Arrange and sew two matching 2½" × 8½" rectangles, one matching 3½" × 8½" rectangle, and two white 1" × 8½" rectangles into a block as shown. Make a total of 25 blocks measuring 8½" square, including seam allowances.

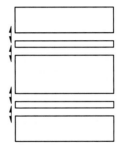 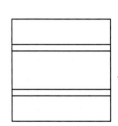

Make 25 blocks,
8½" × 8½".

Assembling the Quilt Top

1. Arrange, rotate, and sew five blocks and four white 1½" × 8½" sashing rectangles into a row as shown. Make a total of five rows measuring 8½" × 44½", including seam allowances.

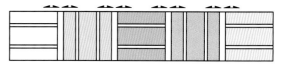

Make 3 rows, 8½" × 44½".

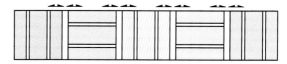

Make 2 rows, 8½" × 44½".

2. Sew five white 1½" × 42" strips together end to end. From this length cut four sashing strips, 44½" long.

3. Referring to the quilt assembly diagram on page 13, sew the five block rows and four sashing strips together. The quilt-top center should measure 44½" square, including seam allowances.

Sashing Savvy

For a less noticeable seam when piecing the white sashing strips together, sew the strips on the diagonal. Place each strip perpendicular to the other and sew from corner to corner. Then trim the seam allowances to ¼" and press them open. Be sure to pin carefully when joining the long sashing strips to the block rows. Check to make sure that the sashing between the blocks aligns visually with the row above.

Adding the Borders

1 Piece the remaining five white 1½" × 42" strips together end to end. From this length, cut two strips, 44½" long, and sew them to the sides of the quilt top.

2 From the remainder of the white strip, cut two strips, 46½" long, and sew them to the top and bottom of the quilt top. The quilt top should measure 46½" square.

3 Piece the five green 3¼" × 42" strips together. From this length, cut two strips, 46½" long, and sew them to the sides of the quilt top.

4 From the remainder of the green strip, cut two strips, 52" long, and sew them to the top and bottom of the quilt top. The completed quilt top should measure 52" square.

Finishing

For more information on any of the finishing steps, go to ShopMartingale.com/HowtoQuilt for free downloadable instructions.

1 Layer the backing, batting, and quilt top; baste the layers together. Hand or machine quilt as desired. Our quilt features machine-quilted radiating petal motifs that create flower designs in the blocks and outer border. The inner border is outline quilted in the ditch.

2 Trim and square up the quilt. Make the binding using the green 2¼"-wide strips and attach it to the quilt.

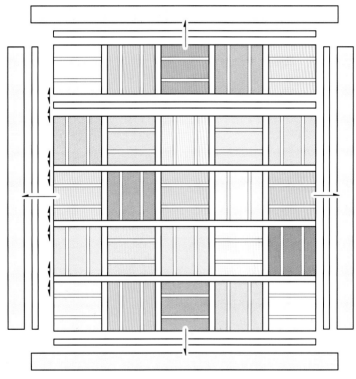

Quilt assembly

Around the Block

FINISHED QUILT: 63" × 77¼" • FINISHED BLOCKS: 2½" × 7½" and 2½" × 5"

Made with the Grow fabric line by Me and My Sister Designs

T raditional quilt patterns done in bright colors always make us smile. Of course, this quilt would also look great in any of your favorite prints and colors. But we encourage you to step outside the box a bit and try using some brights in this one.

Materials

Yardage is based on 42"-wide fabric.

42 squares, 10" × 10", of assorted prints for blocks*
3⅛ yards of white solid for background
⅝ yard of blue diagonal stripe for binding
4⅔ yards of fabric for backing
69" × 84" piece of batting

*A Moda Layer Cake contains 42 squares, 10" × 10".

Cutting

All measurements include ¼" seam allowances.

From each of the print 10" squares, cut:
9 squares, 3" × 3" (378 total; 6 are extra)*

From the white solid, cut:
34 strips, 3" × 42"; crosscut into:
    8 rectangles, 3" × 15½" (A)
    18 rectangles, 3" × 10½" (B)
    66 rectangles, 3" × 8" (C)
    74 rectangles, 3" × 5½" (D)
    6 squares, 3" × 3"

From the blue diagonal stripe, cut:
8 strips, 2¼" × 42"

*You will use only 372 of these.
Choose your favorites!

Making the Blocks

Use a ¼"-wide seam allowance and a small stitch length throughout. Press all seam allowances open.

1 Arrange and sew three print 3" squares together to make a Long block. Make 108 Long blocks measuring 8" × 3", including seam allowances.

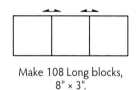

Make 108 Long blocks,
8" × 3".

2 Sew two print 3" squares together to make a Short block. Make 24 Short blocks measuring 5½" × 3", including seam allowances.

Make 24 Short blocks,
5½" × 3".

Assembling the Quilt Top

1 Referring to the row layout diagram below and paying close attention to the order for each row, arrange and sew the blocks, white rectangles, and white squares into 18 rows using the following pieces. Sew the rows together to make one half of the quilt center. Make two halves.

- Row 1: 1 Short block, 2 D rectangles
- Row 2: 1 Long block, 1 C rectangle, 1 D rectangle
- Row 3: 1 Long block, 1 Short block, 1 square, 2 D rectangles
- Row 4: 2 Long blocks, 3 D rectangles
- Row 5: 2 Long blocks, 1 B rectangle, 2 D rectangles
- Row 6: 2 Long blocks, 1 A rectangle, 2 D rectangles
- Row 7: 2 Long blocks, 1 Short block, 2 C rectangles, 2 D rectangles
- Row 8: 3 Long blocks, 1 B rectangle, 1 C rectangle, 2 D rectangles
- Row 9: 3 Long blocks, 1 Short block, 1 square, 2 C rectangles, 2 D rectangles
- Row 10: 4 Long blocks, 2 C rectangles, 3 D rectangles
- Row 11: 4 Long blocks, 1 B rectangle, 2 C rectangles, 2 D rectangles
- Row 12: 4 Long blocks, 1 A rectangle, 2 C rectangles, 2 D rectangles
- Row 13: 4 Long blocks, 1 Short block, 4 C rectangles, 2 D rectangles
- Row 14: 5 Long blocks, 1 B rectangle, 3 C rectangles, 2 D rectangles
- Row 15: 5 Long blocks, 1 Short block, 1 square, 4 C rectangles, 2 D rectangles
- Row 16: 6 Long blocks, 4 C rectangles, 3 D rectangles
- Row 17: 3 Long blocks, 3 Short blocks, 3 B rectangles, 2 C rectangles, 2 D rectangles
- Row 18: 3 Long blocks, 3 Short blocks, 2 B rectangles, 4 C rectangles, 1 D rectangle

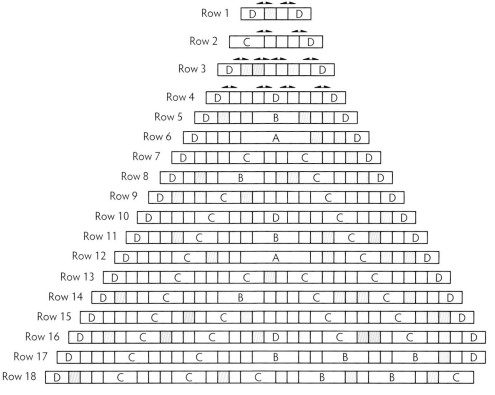

Row layout

2 Sew the two halves together and add two A rectangles to opposite corners as shown. Press all seam allowances open.

Quilt assembly

3 Stay stitch around the quilt a scant 1½" beyond the block points on all sides.

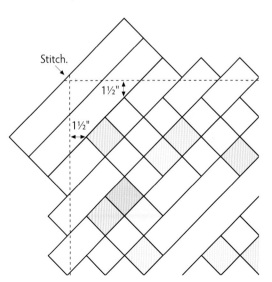

Stitch.

1½"

1½"

4 Trim the quilt 1½" beyond the block points, just outside the stay stitching, on all sides. The completed quilt top should measure 63" × 77¼".

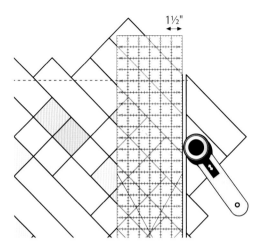

1½"

Finishing

For more information on any of the finishing steps, go to ShopMartingale.com/HowtoQuilt for free downloadable instructions.

1 Layer the backing, batting, and quilt top; baste the layers together. Hand or machine quilt as desired. Our quilt has machine-quilted arcs in the print squares, plus flowers with looping tendrils in the white background.

2 Trim and square up the quilt. Make the binding using the blue 2¼"-wide strips and attach it to the quilt.

Do It Yourself

If you want to try machine quilting, this is an ideal quilt to practice on. The fabric prints in the blocks will disguise any less-than-perfect stitches.

Easy Bake

FINISHED QUILT: 62" × 62" • FINISHED BLOCK: 8½" × 8½"

Made with The Good Life fabric line by Bonnie and Camille

Jumbo-sized slices of Layer Cake squares showcase the larger prints and special fabrics that we love, making this pattern one of our favorites. Everything comes together in a jiff, and that's what makes it so easy to bake.

Materials

Yardage is based on 42"-wide fabric.

36 squares, 10" × 10", of assorted prints for blocks*
⅓ yard of green print for inner border
1 yard of navy print for outer border
⅝ yard of green stripe for binding
3⅞ yards of fabric for backing
68" × 68" square of batting

A Moda Layer Cake contains 42 squares, 10" × 10".

Cutting

All measurements include ¼" seam allowances. Divide the 36 squares into two sets of 18 squares each. Refer to the cutting guides at right when cutting the Layer Cake squares.

From *each* of the 18 print 10" squares from set 1, cut:
1 rectangle, 5" × 9" (18 total)
1 rectangle, 4½" × 5" (18 total)
2 rectangles, 2½" × 4½" (36 total)

From *each* of the 18 print 10" squares from set 2, cut:
1 rectangle, 5" × 9" (18 total)
1 rectangle, 4½" × 5" (18 total)
4 squares, 2½" × 2½" (72 total)*

From the green print, cut:
6 strips, 1½" × 42"

From the navy print, cut:
6 strips, 4¾" × 42"

From the green stripe, cut:
7 strips, 2¼" × 42"

Keep the 2½" squares of the same print together in pairs for the four-patch units.

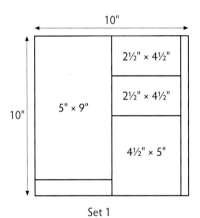

Set 1

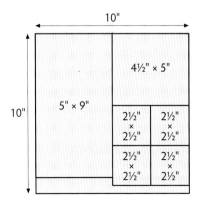

Set 2

Cutting guides

Making the Blocks

Use a ¼"-wide seam allowance and a small stitch length throughout. Press all seam allowances open, unless otherwise noted.

1. For block A, choose four different prints in the following sizes:
   - 1 print rectangle, 5" × 9"
   - 1 print rectangle, 4½" × 5"
   - 1 print rectangle, 2½" × 4½"
   - 1 print rectangle, 2½" × 4½"

2. Arrange the rectangles as shown and sew the block together, beginning with the two smallest rectangles. Make 18 of block A. The blocks should measure 9" square, including seam allowances.

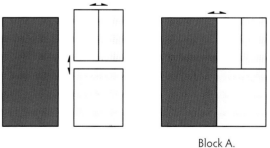

Block A.
Make 18 blocks, 9" × 9".

3. For block B, choose four different prints in the following sizes:
   - 1 print rectangle, 5" × 9"
   - 1 print rectangle, 4½" × 5"
   - 2 matching print squares, 2½" × 2½"
   - 2 matching print squares, 2½" × 2½"

4. Arrange the rectangles and squares as shown and sew the block together, beginning with the squares in the four-patch unit. Make 18 of block B. The blocks should measure 9" square, including seam allowances.

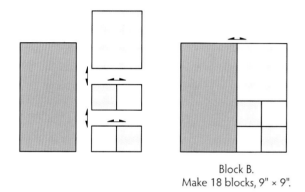

Block B.
Make 18 blocks, 9" × 9".

Assembling the Quilt Top

1. Arrange the blocks into six rows of six blocks each as shown. Sew the blocks into rows. Each row should measure 9" × 51½", including seam allowances.

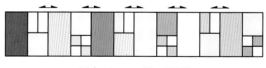

Make 6 rows, 9" × 51½".

2. Rotate three of the six rows so the four-patch units are at the top, as shown in the quilt assembly diagram on page 21. Alternate the rows in the layout and sew them together. The quilt-top center should measure 51½" square, including seam allowances.

Adding the Borders

1 For the inner border, join the six green 1½" × 42" strips together end to end. From this length, cut two strips, 51½" long, and sew them to the sides of the quilt top.

2 From the remainder of the green strip, cut two strips, 53½" long, and sew them to the top and bottom of the quilt top. The quilt top should now measure 53½" square, including seam allowances.

3 For the quilt's outer border, join the six navy 4¾" × 42" strips together end to end. From this length, cut two strips, 53½" long, and sew them to the sides of the quilt top.

4 From the remainder of the navy strip, cut two strips, 62" long, and sew them to the top and bottom of the quilt top. The completed quilt top should measure 62" square.

Finishing

For more information on any of the finishing steps, go to ShopMartingale.com/HowtoQuilt for free downloadable instructions.

1 Layer the backing, batting, and quilt top; baste the layers together. Hand or machine quilt as desired. Our quilt features a machine-quilted overall pattern of large repeating arcs that alternate directions to create a flower design in the blocks.

2 Trim and square up the quilt. Make the binding using the green 2¼"-wide strips and attach it to the quilt.

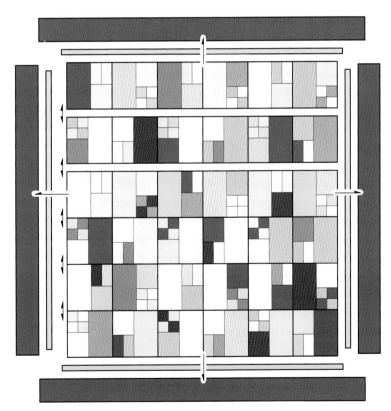

Quilt assembly

Center of Attention

FINISHED QUILT: 76" × 76" · FINISHED BLOCK: 10" × 10"

Made with the Confetti fabric line by Me and My Sister Designs

Materials

Yardage is based on 42"-wide fabric.

36 strips, 1½" × 42", of assorted prints for blocks
36 squares, 10" × 10", of assorted prints for blocks*
⅝ yard of green print for inner border
⅝ yard of turquoise print for middle border
1⅛ yards of multicolored geometric print for
    outer border
⅝ yard of pink dot for binding
6⅞ yards of fabric for backing**
82" × 82" square of batting

A Moda Layer Cake contains 42 squares, 10" × 10".

**If your fabric is at least 42" wide after removing
selvages, 4⅝ yards will be enough for backing.*

Cutting

*All measurements include ¼" seam allowances.
Keep like triangles together.*

From *each* of the print 1½" × 42" strips, cut:
2 strips, 1½" × 17" (72 total)

From *each* of the print 10" squares, cut:
2 triangles by cutting the square in half diagonally
    once (72 total)

From the green print, cut:
7 strips, 2½" × 42"

From the turquoise print, cut:
7 strips, 2½" × 42"

From the multicolored geometric print, cut:
8 strips, 4¼" × 42"

From the pink dot, cut:
8 strips, 2¼" × 42"

Making the Blocks

Use a ¼"-wide seam allowance and a small stitch
length throughout. Press all seam allowances open,
unless otherwise noted.

1 Sew two print 1½" × 17" strips together along
the long edges to make the block center. Make
36 block centers.

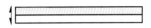

Make 36 block centers.

2 Sew a block center between two matching
triangles as shown. Make 36.

 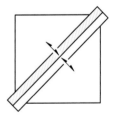

Make 36.

3 Trim the blocks to 10½" square, making sure
the seam between the two strips intersects
the corners of the block.

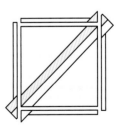

Trim to 10½" × 10½".

Assembling the Quilt Top

Referring to the quilt assembly diagram on page 25, arrange the blocks in six rows of six blocks each. Sew the blocks into rows and then sew the rows together. The quilt center should measure 60½" square, including seam allowances.

Adding the Borders

1 For the inner border, join the seven green 2½" × 42" strips together end to end. From this length, cut two strips, 60½" long, and sew them to the sides of the quilt center.

2 From the remainder of the green strip, cut two strips, 64½" long, and sew them to the top and bottom of the quilt center. The quilt top should now measure 64½" square, including seam allowances.

3 For the middle border, piece the seven turquoise 2½" × 42" strips together end to end. From this length, cut two strips, 64½" long, and sew them to the sides of the quilt top.

So Many Options

This quilt has so much potential for fun! You could use just two fabrics for the block centers to coordinate with your decor or to highlight someone's favorite colors. The fabrics could be prints or solids. When it comes to setting the blocks together, wouldn't it be fun to orient them so that the diagonal block centers create diamonds? You could even make a center diamond with echoing diamonds around it, like a Log Cabin quilt barn raising setting.

4 From the remainder of the turquoise strip, cut two strips, 68½" long, and sew them to the top and bottom of the quilt top. The quilt top should now measure 68½" square, including seam allowances.

5 For the outer border, join the eight multicolored 4¼" × 42" strips together end to end. From this length, cut two strips, 68½" long, and sew them to the sides of the quilt top.

6 From the remainder of the multicolored strip, cut two strips, 76" long, and sew them to the top and bottom of the quilt top. The completed quilt top should measure 76" square.

Finishing

For more information on any of the finishing steps, go to ShopMartingale.com/HowtoQuilt for free downloadable instructions.

1 Layer the backing, batting, and quilt top; baste the layers together. Hand or machine quilt as desired. Our quilt features machine-quilted loops in the diagonal pieces and a curving feather design in every other diagonal row of the triangles. The alternate triangles feature straight parallel lines.

2 Trim and square up the quilt. Make the binding using the pink 2¼"-wide strips and attach it to the quilt.

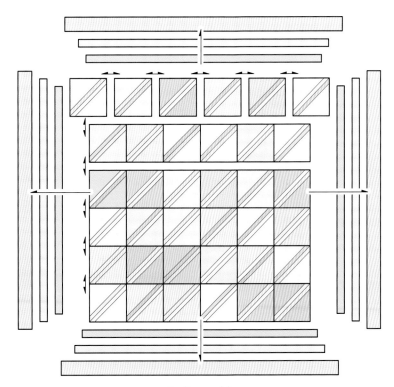

Quilt assembly

Flipping Out

FINISHED QUILT: 80½" × 100½" • FINISHED BLOCK: 20" × 20"

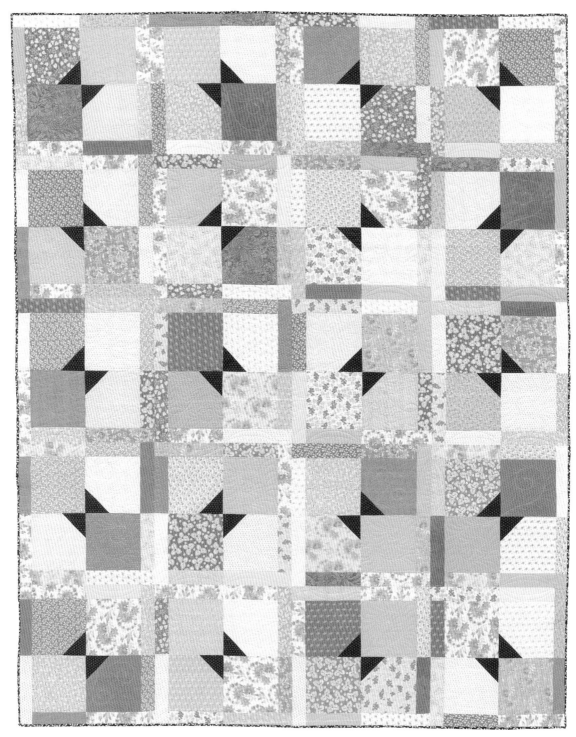

Made with the Hazel and Plum fabric line by Fig Tree and Co.

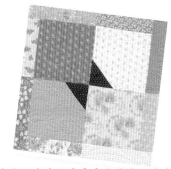

You'll flip over this quilt! Choose a bold contrasting color for the corner "flips" to see a dramatic effect. Then pair your bold color with two Layer Cakes to make a super-sized project. It's the perfect recipe for a large crowd.

Materials

Yardage is based on 42"-wide fabric.

40 strips, 2½" × 42", of assorted prints for blocks*
80 squares, 10" × 10", of assorted prints for blocks**
⅝ yard of brown tone on tone for blocks
¾ yard of brown print for binding
7½ yards of fabric for backing
89" × 109" piece of batting

A Moda Jelly Roll contains 40 strips, 2½" × 42".

**A Moda Layer Cake contains 42 squares, 10" × 10".*

Cutting

All measurements include ¼" seam allowances.

From *each* of the print 2½" × 42" strips, cut:
2 rectangles, 2½" × 10½" (80 total)
2 rectangles, 2½" × 8½" (80 total)

From *each* of the print 10" squares, cut:
1 square, 8½" × 8½" (80 total)

From the brown tone on tone, cut:
4 strips, 4" × 42"; crosscut into 40 squares, 4" × 4"

From the brown print, cut:
10 strips, 2¼" × 42"

Making the Blocks

Use a ¼"-wide seam allowance and a small stitch length throughout. Press all seam allowances open.

1 Arrange and sew one print 2½" × 8½" rectangle to the side of a print 8½" square. Sew a different print 2½" × 10½" rectangle to the bottom to make a unit that measures 10½" square. Make 80 units.

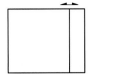

Make 80 units,
10½" × 10½".

2 Divide the 80 units into two sets of 40 each. Put one of these sets aside.

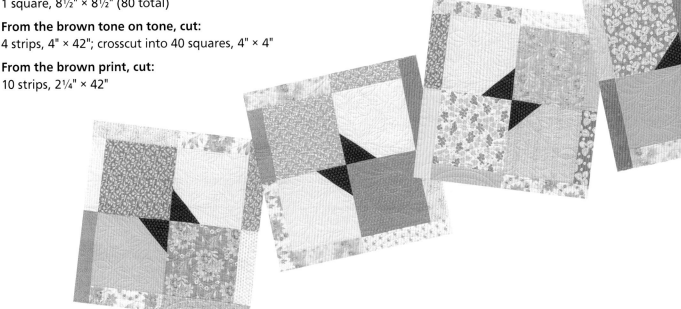

3 Draw a diagonal line from corner to corner on the wrong side of each brown tone-on-tone 4" square. With right sides together, place a marked square on the corner of a unit as shown. Stitch on the marked line and then trim the corner, leaving a ¼" seam allowance. Make 40 units.

Make 40 units, 10½" × 10½".

4 Arrange two of the units set aside in step 2 and two units from step 3 as shown. Sew the units together to make a block measuring 20½" square, including seam allowances. Make a total of 20 blocks.

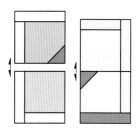 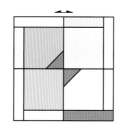

Make 20 blocks, 20½" × 20½".

Fringe Benefit

The triangles trimmed from the corners of the block units can easily be sewn together to create half-square-triangle units for another project. If you'd like to sew them while making the block units in step 3 above, simply draw a second line ½" from the first diagonal line. Sew on both lines and then cut between the stitched lines. Press the half-square-triangle units, then trim to 3" square for a 2½" finished unit. You'll have 40 units to play with.

Assembling the Quilt Top

Referring to the quilt assembly diagram below, arrange the blocks into five rows of four blocks each, rotating them as shown. Sew the blocks into rows and then sew the rows together to complete the quilt top. The completed quilt top should measure 80½" × 100½".

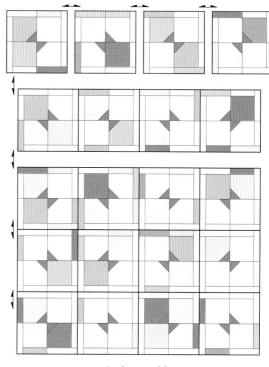

Quilt assembly

Finishing

For more information on any of the finishing steps, go to ShopMartingale.com/HowtoQuilt for free downloadable instructions.

1 Layer the backing, batting, and quilt top; baste the layers together. Hand or machine quilt as desired. Our quilt features leaf shapes, feathered spiral designs, and large and small arcs filled with figure eights. The "flips" are outlined with quilting in the ditch.

2 Trim and square up the quilt. Make the binding using the brown 2¼"-wide strips and attach it to the quilt.

Ten Cents

FINISHED QUILT: 48½" × 53" • FINISHED BLOCK: 8" × 8"

Made with the Authentic Etc. fabric line by Sweetwater

Break the speed limit making these superlarge half-square-triangle blocks! We love making triangle blocks, and if they happen to have a few "speed bumps" between them, we don't mind.

Materials

Yardage is based on 42"-wide fabric.

36 squares, 10" × 10", of assorted prints for blocks*
⅞ yard of gray print for sashing and binding
3⅛ yards of fabric for backing
55" × 59" piece of batting

A Moda Layer Cake contains 42 squares, 10" × 10".

Cutting

All measurements include ¼" seam allowances.

From the gray print, cut:
5 strips, 2" × 42"; crosscut into 18 rectangles,
    2" × 8½"
6 strips, 2¼" × 42"

Making the Blocks

Use a ¼"-wide seam allowance and a small stitch length throughout. Press all seam allowances open.

1 Divide the 36 squares into 18 pairs of light and dark values or contrasting prints.

2 Draw a diagonal line from corner to corner on the wrong side of a square from one pair. With right sides together, layer the marked and unmarked squares. Stitch ¼" from each side of the drawn line. Cut apart on the marked line and press to make two matching half-square-triangle blocks. Trim the blocks to 8½" square. Make a total of 36 blocks.

8½"

8½"

Make 36 blocks.

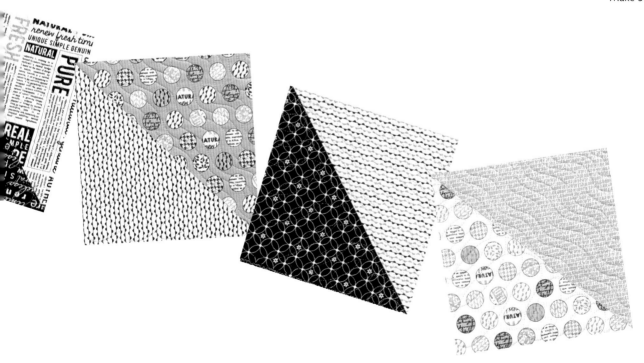

Assembling the Quilt Top

Arrange the blocks in six vertical rows of six blocks each, with three gray 2" × 8½" sashing rectangles in each row as shown. The placement of the gray rectangles changes from row to row. Sew the blocks and rectangles into rows, and then sew the rows together to complete the quilt top. The completed quilt top should measure 48½" × 53".

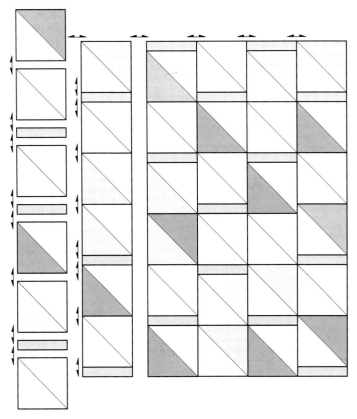

Quilt assembly

Finishing

For more information on any of the finishing steps, go to ShopMartingale.com/HowtoQuilt for free downloadable instructions.

1. Layer the backing, batting, and quilt top; baste the layers together. Hand or machine quilt as desired. Our quilt is machine quilted with an alternating pattern of elongated loops and parallel wavy lines.

2. Trim and square up the quilt. Make the binding using the gray 2¼"-wide strips and attach it to the quilt.

On the 45

FINISHED QUILT: 51½" × 69"

Made with the Giggles fabric line by Me and My Sister Designs

Who doesn't love a great zigzag pattern? Slice your Layer Cake into three equal portions before mixing and serving up this quilt. The ingredients are simple and the results are delectable!

Materials

Yardage is based on 42"-wide fabric.

32 squares, 10" × 10", of assorted prints for rows*
2⅞ yards of white solid for rows and border
⅝ yard of turquoise print for binding
3¼ yards of fabric for backing
58" × 75" piece of batting
Ruler with 45° angle marking

A Moda Layer Cake contains 42 squares, 10" × 10".

Cutting

All measurements include ¼" seam allowances. Keep like prints together.

From *each* of the print 10" squares, cut:
3 rectangles, 3" × 9½" (96 total)

From the white solid, cut:
10 strips, 7½" × 42"; crosscut into 120 rectangles, 3" × 7½"
3 strips, 4¾" × 42"

From the turquoise print, cut:
7 strips, 2¼" × 42"

Assembling the Rows

Use a ¼"-wide seam allowance and a small stitch length throughout. Press all seam allowances open, unless otherwise noted.

1 To make one strip, choose four assorted print 3" × 9½" rectangles and five white 3" × 7½" rectangles.

2 On the wrong side of a print 3" × 9½" rectangle, align the 45° line of the ruler with the left edge and upper-left corner as shown and draw a diagonal line. Repeat to draw a diagonal line on all four print 3" × 9½" rectangles and on four of the white 3" × 7½" rectangles.

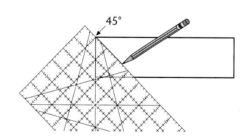

3 With right sides together, place a print rectangle perpendicular to the unmarked white rectangle as shown. Sew on the drawn line. You may want to pin this seam and then open it up to make sure that you are flipping in the correct direction before sewing. Trim the seam allowance to ¼" and press.

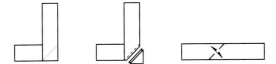

4 Continue sewing and alternating marked white and print rectangles to complete one pieced strip measuring 3" × 51½", including seam allowances. Make three identical strips. Press all seam allowances open.

Make 3 matching strips, 3" × 51½".

5 Sew the three strips together to make row 1. The row should measure 8" × 51½", including seam allowances.

6 Repeat steps 1–5 to make rows 3, 5, and 7.

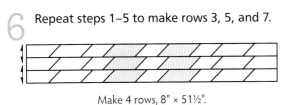

Make 4 rows, 8" × 51½".

7 Repeat steps 1–4 to make three matching strips each for rows 2, 4, 6, and 8, with two changes: First, reverse the angle of the drawn line in step 2, as shown below. Second, layer the top rectangle downward rather than upward in step 3 when sewing them together.

8 Join three matching strips for each row. Make a total of four rows.

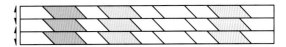

Make 4 rows, 8" × 51½".

More Fun

After making this quilt, you'll have an abundance of leftover triangles that you can sew into half-square-triangle units. If you sew all of them, you'll have 192 units, enough to make a sweet doll quilt or table topper. Trim the units to 2" square for 1½" finished units.

Assembling the Quilt Top

1 Sew the rows together as shown in the quilt assembly diagram below.

2 Sew the three white 4¾" × 42" strips together end to end. From this length, cut two strips, 51½" long, and sew them to the top and bottom of the quilt. The completed quilt top should measure 51½" × 69".

Finishing

For more information on any of the finishing steps, go to ShopMartingale.com/HowtoQuilt for free downloadable instructions.

1 Layer the backing, batting, and quilt top; baste the layers together. Hand or machine quilt as desired. Our quilt has machine-quilted designs of swirls and chains of leaf shapes. The print pieces are outline quilted in the ditch. The top and bottom borders feature a leafy vine and tendrils.

2 Trim and square up the quilt. Make the binding using the turquoise 2¼"-wide strips and attach it to the quilt.

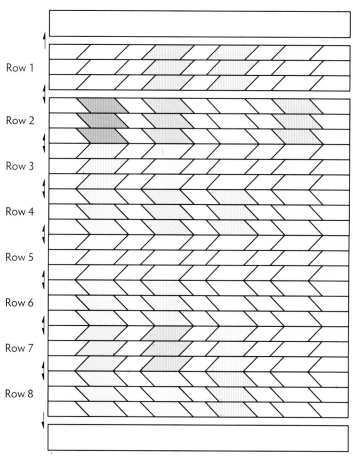

Quilt assembly

Stacks

FINISHED QUILT: 64½" × 72½" • FINISHED BLOCK: 8" × 8"

Made with the Frolic! fabric line by Me and My Sister Designs

Pair a print Layer Cake with a solid Layer Cake and you've just made this quilt even easier. Stack all your squares into pairs and before you know it, you'll have stacked, cut, and sewn your way to a finished quilt.

Materials

Yardage is based on 42"-wide fabric.

36 squares, 10" × 10", of assorted prints for blocks
36 squares, 10" × 10", of white solid for blocks
⅝ yard of black-and-white stripe for binding
4 yards of fabric for backing
71" × 79" piece of batting

A Moda Layer Cake contains 42 squares, 10" × 10".

Cutting

All measurements include ¼" seam allowances.

From the black-and-white stripe, cut:
8 strips, 2¼" × 42"

Cutting the Blocks

1 Stack one print and one white square together so that all edges are even. Make 36 stacks.

2 Align the 1" line of a rotary ruler with the corners of two layered squares and cut along the diagonal of the stack as shown to create a pair of triangles. Move the triangles aside.

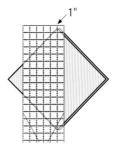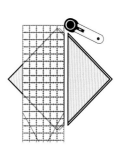

3 Rotate the remainder of the stack, being careful not to shift the fabric layers, and align the 1" line of your ruler with the corners as before. Cut along the diagonal as shown. You'll have four triangles and two center strips.

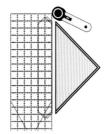

4 Repeat steps 2 and 3 to cut all 36 of the stacks.

Making the Blocks

Use a ¼"-wide seam allowance and a small stitch length throughout. Press all seam allowances open.

1 Arrange two contrasting print triangles and one white center strip as shown. Fold each piece in half and crease to find the center. Align the centers and sew the white center strip between the two triangles. Trim the block to 8½" square, keeping the center strip aligned in the center of the block. See "Trim to Perfection," below. Make 36 blocks.

Make 36 blocks;
trim to 8½" × 8½".

2 Arrange two white triangles and one print center strip as shown. Fold each piece in half and crease to find the center. Align the centers and sew the print center strip between the two white triangles. Trim the block to 8½" square, keeping the print strip centered in the block. Make 36 blocks.

Make 36 blocks;
trim to 8½" × 8½".

Trim to Perfection

When trimming the first side of the block, make sure that the 45° angle line on your ruler bisects the center strip exactly. The center strip should be 1½" wide after sewing, so the angle line should be ¾" away from the seam. A 8½" square ruler is easiest to use, but if you don't have one, other rulers will also work.

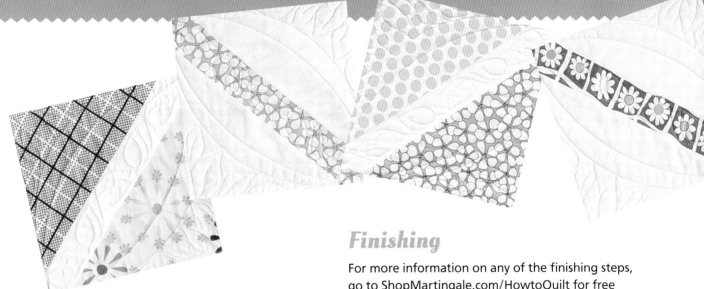

Assembling the Quilt Top

Referring to the quilt assembly diagram below, rotate and arrange the blocks in nine rows of eight blocks each. Sew the blocks into rows. The rows should measure 8½" × 64½", including seam allowances. Sew the rows together to complete the quilt top. The completed quilt top should measure 64½" × 72½".

Finishing

For more information on any of the finishing steps, go to ShopMartingale.com/HowtoQuilt for free downloadable instructions.

1 Layer the backing, batting, and quilt top; baste the layers together. Hand or machine quilt as desired. Our quilt is machine quilted with large arcs and leaf shapes. Leaves and vines fill the narrow rectangle areas.

2 Trim and square up the quilt. Make the binding using the black-and-white 2¼"-wide strips and attach it to the quilt.

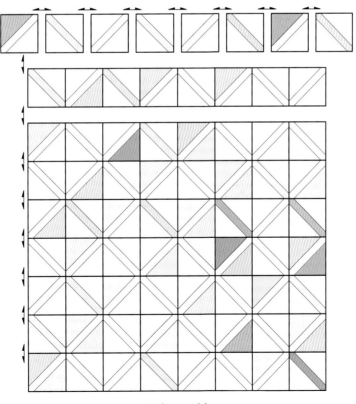

Quilt assembly

Friendship

FINISHED QUILT: **46½" × 58½"** • FINISHED BLOCK: **6" × 6"**

Made with the Flower Mill fabric line by Corey Yoder

Oh my stars! Who knew a Layer Cake could be transformed into a celestial blanket? Perfect for a slumber party or a signature quilt, this pattern is a use-it-all-up recipe. Layer Cake squares appear in the border as well as in the quilt center—no leftovers!

Materials

Yardage is based on 42"-wide fabric.

2⅛ yards of white solid for blocks and inner border
36 squares, 10" × 10", of assorted prints for blocks and outer border*
½ yard of pink print for binding
3 yards of fabric for backing
53" × 65" piece of batting

*A Moda Layer Cake contains 42 squares, 10" × 10".

Cutting

All measurements include ¼" seam allowances. Keep like prints together.

From the white solid, cut:
15 strips, 2⅞" × 42"; crosscut into 192 squares, 2⅞" × 2⅞"
3 strips, 2½" × 42"; crosscut into 48 squares, 2½" × 2½"
5 strips, 3½" × 42"

From *each* of the print 10" squares, cut:
6 squares, 2⅞" × 2⅞" (216 total; 24 are extra)*
1 rectangle, 2½" × 9" (36 total; 8 are extra)

From the pink print, cut:
6 strips, 2¼" × 42"

*You will use only 192 of these. Choose your favorites!

Making the Blocks

Use a ¼"-wide seam allowance and a small stitch length throughout. Press all seam allowances open, unless otherwise noted.

1 For one block, choose:
   • 4 matching print squares, 2⅞" × 2⅞"
   • 4 white squares, 2⅞" × 2⅞"
   • 1 white square, 2½" × 2½"

2 Draw a diagonal line on the wrong side of each of the white 2⅞" squares. With right sides together, layer a marked square with a print 2⅞" square, aligning the edges. Stitch ¼" from each side of the drawn line. Cut apart on the marked line and press to make two identical half-square-triangle units. Make eight units measuring 2½" square.

Make 8 units, 2½" × 2½".

3 Arrange and sew the eight matching half-square-triangle units and the white 2½" square into rows as shown. Sew the rows together to complete the block. Make 33 two-color blocks measuring 6½" square.

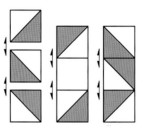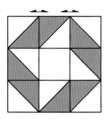

Make 33 blocks,
6½" × 6½".

4 Repeat step 2 with the remaining white and print 2⅞" squares. Make a total of 120 half-square-triangle units.

5 Choose an assortment of eight half-square-triangle units and repeat step 3 to make a scrappy block. Make 15 scrappy blocks measuring 6½" square.

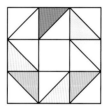

Make 15 blocks,
6½" × 6½".

Assembling the Quilt Top

Arrange the blocks into eight rows of six blocks each, referring to the quilt assembly diagram on page 43. The scrappy blocks are placed randomly in the layout. Sew the blocks into rows and sew the rows together to make the quilt center. The quilt center should measure 36½" × 48½", including seam allowances.

Adding the Borders

1 For the first border, join the five white 3½" × 42" strips together end to end. From this length, cut two strips, 48½" long, and sew them to the sides of the quilt top.

2 From the remainder of the white strip, cut two strips, 42½" long, and sew them to the top and bottom of the quilt top. The quilt top should measure 42½" × 54½".

3 For the outer border, join 28 print 2½" × 9" rectangles end to end. From this length, cut two strips, 54½" long, and sew them to the sides of the quilt top.

4 From the remainder of the pieced strip, cut two strips, 46½" long, and sew them to the top and bottom of the quilt. The completed quilt top should measure 46½" × 58½".

Finishing

For more information on any of the finishing steps, go to ShopMartingale.com/HowtoQuilt for free downloadable instructions.

1 Layer the backing, batting, and quilt top; baste the layers together. Hand or machine quilt as desired. Our quilt is machine quilted with designs that include spirals, loops, and curved lines.

2 Trim and square up the quilt. Make the binding using the pink 2¼"-wide strips and attach it to the quilt.

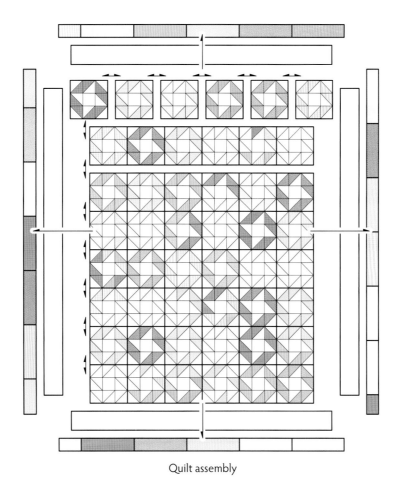

Quilt assembly

Daybreak

FINISHED QUILT: 61" × 68½" • FINISHED BLOCK: 8½" × 8½"

Made with the Good Morning fabric line by Me and My Sister Designs

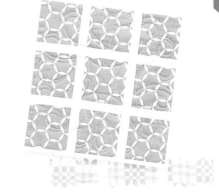

N ine Patch blocks are "exploded" and paired with larger panels of fabric to create a modern design. Simple recipes are sometimes the best, and they never get old. We hope this quilt becomes a family favorite.

Materials

Yardage is based on 42"-wide fabric.

20 squares, 10" × 10", of assorted prints for blocks*
2¼ yards of white solid for blocks, sashing, and border
⅓ yard *each of 5 florals for blocks**
⅝ yard of blue print for binding
3¾ yards of fabric for backing
67" × 75" piece of batting

*A Moda Layer Cake contains 42 squares, 10" × 10".
Our quilt includes 4 squares each of green, purple,
blue, pink, and orange.*

**Our quilt includes 1 each of green, purple, blue,
pink, and orange.*

Cutting

*All measurements include ¼" seam allowances.
Keep like prints together.*

From *each* of the print 10" squares, cut:
3 rectangles, 3" × 9" (60 total)

From the white solid, cut:
13 strips, 3½" × 42"
3 strips, 9" × 42"; crosscut into:
    20 strips, 1½" × 9"
    80 strips, 1" × 9"

From *each* of the florals, cut:
1 rectangle, 9" × 24½" (5 total)

From the blue print, cut:
7 strips, 2¼" × 42"

Making the Blocks

Use a ¼"-wide seam allowance and a small stitch length throughout. Press all seam allowances open, unless otherwise noted.

1 Arrange and sew three matching print 3" × 9" rectangles and two white 1" × 9" strips together as shown.

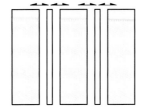 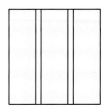

2 Rotate the unit and cut it into three segments, each measuring 3" × 9".

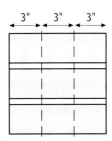 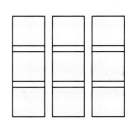

Cut 3 segments,
3" × 9".

3 Sew two white 1" × 9" strips between the segments from step 2 as shown to complete the block. Make a total of 20 blocks measuring 9" square, including seam allowances.

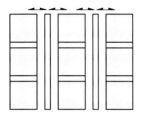 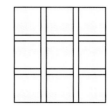

Make 20 blocks, 9" × 9".

Assembling the Quilt Top

1 Arrange the blocks, floral 9" × 24½" rectangles, and white 1½" × 9" strips into five columns as shown in the quilt assembly diagram on page 47. There should be four blocks, one floral rectangle, and four white strips in each row. Sew the pieces into columns measuring 9" × 62½", including seam allowances.

2 Join seven of the white 3½" × 42" strips together end to end. From this length, cut four strips, 62½" long, for sashing. Set the remainder of the strip aside for the border.

3 Arrange and sew the five columns and four white sashing strips together, referring to the quilt assembly diagram. The quilt center should measure 55" × 62½", including seam allowances.

4 Join the six white 3½" × 42" strips and the remaining 3½"-wide strip from the sashing together end to end. From this length, cut two strips, 62½" long, and sew them to the sides of the quilt center.

Scrappy Suggestion

As an alternative to the unpieced floral rectangle in each row, you could instead sew together prints or solids from your stash to create a pieced unit. The options are many. The pieced strip just needs to measure the same as the floral rectangle called for in the instructions, 9" x 24½".

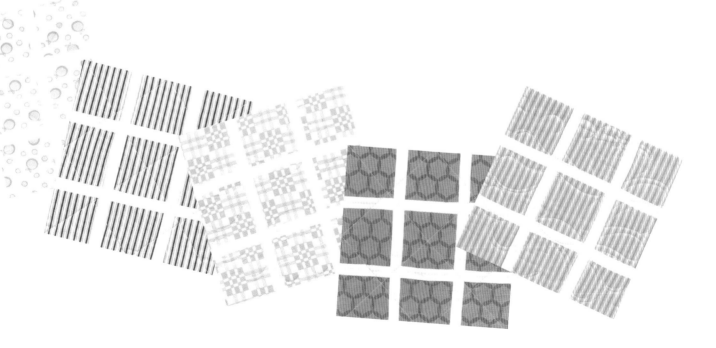

5 From the remainder of the white strip, cut two strips, 61"
long, and sew them to the top and bottom of the quilt top.
The completed quilt top should measure 61" × 68½".

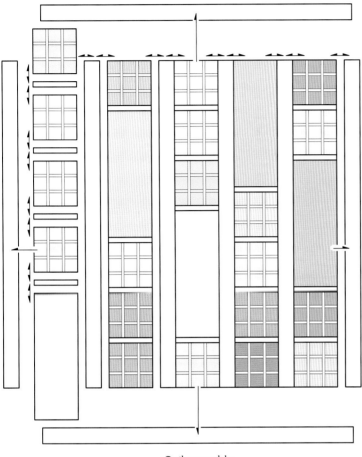

Quilt assembly

Finishing

For more information on any of the finishing steps, go to
ShopMartingale.com/HowtoQuilt for free downloadable
instructions.

1 Layer the backing, batting, and quilt top; baste the layers
together. Hand or machine quilt as desired. Our quilt
features a machine-quilted diagonal grid and swirls in the print
areas, with parallel lines in the white areas.

2 Trim and square up the quilt. Make the binding using
the blue 2¼"-wide strips and attach it to the quilt.

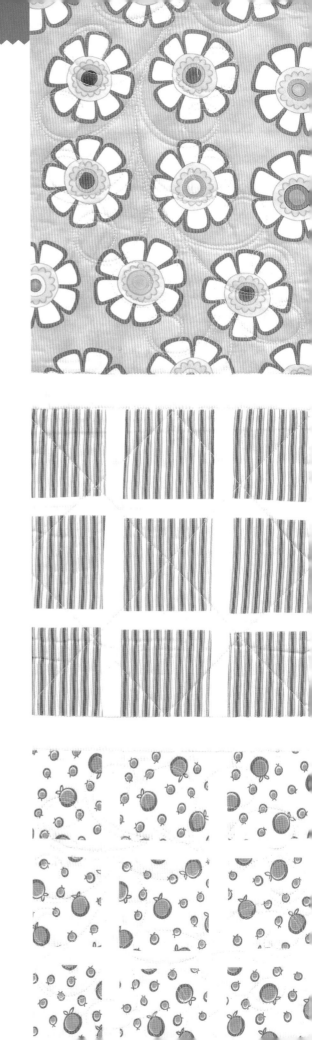

About the Authors

Acknowledgment

Our quilts were machine quilted by the very talented Sharon Elsberry, who has a business called Akamai Quilts. Her quilting designs bring our quilts to life and are truly the icing on the cake!

~Barbara and Mary

Sisters **Barbara Groves** and **Mary Jacobson** make up the popular design team of Me and My Sister Designs, based in Tempe, Arizona. Their belief in fast, fun, and easy designs can be seen in the quilts created for their pattern company and in their fabric designs for Moda. The authors of several best-selling books, Barbara and Mary share more of their quick and pretty patterns in *12-Pack Quilts, Simple Quilts from Me and My Sister Designs,* and *Easy Layer-Cake Quilts.* To learn more, visit them at MeandMySisterDesigns.com.

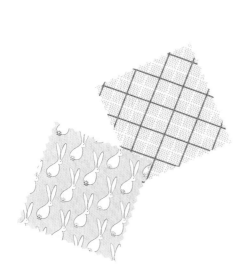